Walks, Trails, and Parks on Vashon Island

John H. Gerstle
and
Susan G. Sullivan

THIRD EDITION

Vashon Island
February 2007

Walks, Trails, and Parks on Vashon Island

Third edition

Front Cover: Gold Beach and Point Robinson lie in the distance along the southwest shore of Maury Island. Photo taken north of Sandy Shores.
Back cover: There are major stands of madrone on Maury Island.

Cover photographs ©Ray Pfortner
pfortner@centurytel.net

Layout and publishing by
Capturing Memories
www.capturingmemories.com

Printed in the U.S.A.
ISBN: 0-9727759-8-6
US Copyright Office: TX 5-866-837

DEDICATION

This guide, *Walks, Trails, and Parks on Vashon Island*, is dedicated to the Vashon Park District. We applaud its mission of developing and preserving passive and active recreation resources as well as protecting the rural and natural qualities of our Island. Vashon Parks is only one of our many angel groups which include King County, the Island's Audubon Society, the Vashon-Maury Island Land Trust, Vashon Forest Stewards, and the many islanders who care for this quiet, picturesque, funky island.

This book is a gift from the authors and photographers to the Vashon Park District which has undertaken its publication. Net proceeds from its sales will go to the Vashon Park District.

Vashon-Maury Island Park District
17130 Vashon Highway SW
P.O. Box 1553
Vashon, WA 98070
(206) 463-9602
www.vashonparkdistrict.org

ACKNOWLEDGEMENTS

The authors acknowledge Jill and Murray Andrews, Pat Christopherson, May Gerstle, Alan Huggins, Brian and Anne O'Leary, and Marie Stanislaw for their support on beach walks. The authors thank Wendy Braicks, Julie Burman, Niki McBride, David Frank, Shelley Means, and Scott Snyder for their help with resource material. Also we thank Shirley Ferris for inspiration, photographs accompanying the text, and a review of the manuscript; Ray Pfortner for the front and back cover photographs; Doug Huizinga for help with trail maps; and Pat Sullivan for inspiration.

The authors are deeply indebted to Ann Spiers for generous and inspired ideas and invaluable editing help and to Rayna Holtz for providing many corrections and additions as well as ideas for inclusion in the second edition.

TABLE OF CONTENTS

MIXED TRAIL AND STREET WALKS 55

STREET WALKS 58

REFERENCES 64

MAPS

I
INTRODUCTION

WELCOME TO THE PLEASURES OF EXPLORING quiet Vashon Island. Noted for its "funky rurality," Vashon Island is about 13 miles long and four miles wide. Maury Island, immediately to the east of Vashon, is about five miles long and roughly two miles wide. Vashon and Maury Islands, collectively called the Island in this guide, are connected by an isthmus. The Island is 37 square miles in area and is bordered by two major cities, Seattle and Tacoma. Fifty miles of beachfront, almost one-half of all shoreline in King County, circle the Island.

The climate is characterized by mild winters and cool summers. High temperatures, averaging 70 degrees, occur from July through September. While Vashon's average rainfall is 46 inches per year, its northwest side receives as much as 50% more than Maury's east side. Peak rainfall usually occurs from November through February.

The Island's geologic features result from a series of glaciations during Pleistocene time from about 2 million to 10,000 years ago. The last glaciation, peaking about 15,000 years ago, is called the Vashon Stade of the Fraser Glaciation.

Historically, the Island was occupied by the S'Homamish Tribe, a band of the Puyallup Tribe of Indians (Ref. 16). Native American groups had established lodges and used the Island seasonally for hunting and gathering (Ref. 11). An archeological dig on Vashon's Jensen Point in 1996 demonstrates that the tribes used the site for fish processing and summer camp as long as 1000 years ago (Ref. 16). Evidence at other Island locales suggests Native American presence back to at least 8000 years (Ref. 16).

Introduction

The 1854 Medicine Creek Treaty removed the Island's Native Americans from the Island. They were located eventually on the Puyallup Reservation across Puget Sound at Tacoma. In 1857, the number of S'Homamish was estimated to be only 441 (Ref. 2), since their population had been decimated by epidemics from diseases borne by white newcomers.

Vashon Island was named by British explorer Captain George Vancouver in 1792 on his "Voyage of Discovery." He named the Island after his friend James Vashon, who later became an admiral. In 1841, Maury Island was named by US Navy Lieutenant Charles Wilkes while surveying the area in order to reinforce the United States' claim to Puget Sound. He named Maury Island after William Maury, a survey member.

In the early 1850s, logging preceded the first white settlers. In 1857, the Island was surveyed. The surveyors found some very large trees; one of the largest, a cedar eight feet in diameter, was near what is now Cedarhurst Road. While the Island was heavily forested before the white settlers, much of the forest cover had been burned. Some fires had been caused by lightning strikes, but it is probable that fires were also set by Native Americans seeking to maintain open spaces for edible plants (Ref. 18). Logging of the Island has continued to the present time, with the second growth being heavily logged in the 1940s and 1950s and third growth logged in 1980s and 1990s. Currently, interest is increasing in ecological forestry to improve the health of the remaining 15,000 acres of forest.

The Homestead Act of 1862 allowed filing of land claims for ownership by private individuals. In 1877, the first permanent non-native settlers came to the Island. In the 1800s and early 1900s, the Island became an agricultural area, a site for boat building, and a destination for summer cabin dwellers. Its shoreline communities were linked by water to each other and the mainland.

In the early 1900s, the Island became famous for its strawberries. Vashon's Mukai family developed a straw-

4

berry-packaging method for the frozen fruit market. Their processing plant shipped Island strawberries worldwide. Greenhouses, including Beall Greenhouse later famous for its roses and orchids, sent vegetables to Seattle and Alaska (Ref. 14).

In 1963, K2 Skis built its headquarters and fiberglass-ski factory. As the Island approached the 21st century, land use shifted from farming to residential for families who commute for work off Island, or who work in Island businesses such as town shops, inns and bed & breakfasts, school district, construction, and small factories (Ref. 9). There is a flourishing arts community and the computer age facilitates small on-Island businesses. A new generation of organic farmers supplies customers through subscription farming, Saturday markets, and special-product markets.

In 1920, the US Census counted the population of Vashon-Maury as 2,801 (Ref. 2). By 2000, the population reached 10,300. The first car ferry service started in 1916 (Des Moines to Portage). Early shoreline communities were served by a fleet of small ferries called the Mosquito Fleet. These boats landed at docks around the Island (Ref. 6). On beach walks, you will see the remains of these docks, now picturesque pilings often used as perches by cormorants. In 1951, the Washington State Ferry System began regular service (Ref. 2). In the more recent past, a bridge proposal seems to arise every 15 or 20 years. In 1991, more than 1,000 Islanders successfully protested a bridge that would link the Island to the mainland. Inconvenience of ferry commuting, lack of water sources, and zoning contribute to the Island's relatively small population growth, retention of green space, and undeveloped shoreline.

Anyone interested in learning more about Island history will enjoy visiting the Vashon-Maury Island Heritage Museum at 10105 SW Bank Road. Call (206) 567-0555 for operating hours, since they change seasonally.

II
WILDLIFE

O NLY BY WALKING CAN ONE CAN SEE much more of the
Island's wildlife. Bald eagles have staged a remark-
able recovery and are frequently seen on trees, snags, or
pilings overlooking the beaches. Watch for great blue
herons patiently seeking a meal at the water's edge. The
Island's sandy, gravelly, and cobblestone shoreline
attracts crows and gulls, mostly glaucous-winged gulls
(Ref. 8). Other birds include Canada geese, cormorants,
golden-eyes, bufflehead, grebes, mallards, ospreys, purple martins, sandpipers, scoters, sparrows, swallows,
wigeons, and wood ducks (Ref. 1). Notice holes in the
bare cliff faces. These may be belted kingfisher nests. A
sure give-away is the parent kingfisher scolding you from
a nearby tree. Northern rough-winged swallows and pigeon guillemots also nest in the cliffs. All told, the Vashon-Maury Island Audubon Society has recorded more
than 200 bird species on the Island.

In the waters around the Island, seals, sea lions, and, on
occasion, orca whales travel. River otters forage in the
vegetation bordering the beaches. Walking on the beach
at low tides allows you to explore tide pools and observe
sea stars, crabs, and anemones. Children can look for
beach glass and driftwood. Beach walkers, however,
should take care to minimize harm to the intertidal habitat
by replacing overturned rocks and by not taking home
sea creatures. Do look, smell, and listen, but touch only
lightly.

Crab species include green shore crab, black-clawed
crab, graceful decorator crab, Dungeness crab and red
rock crab. Native littleneck, Japanese or Manila littleneck, and butter clams are the most numerous clam
species. Other bivalves are cockles, softshells, horse

clams, macomas, jackknife clams, bay mussels, horse mussels, geoducks, and pink scallops.

The sheltered waters of Puget Sound provide important habitat for salmon and other fish species. Large seaweed grows on rocky shores. Minute seaweed grows on eelgrass blades on the quieter, sandier beaches. Watch for cockles, moon snails, and sand dollars. The eelgrass beds help protect forage fish such as Pacific herring and surf smelt, which spawn on sandy beaches, as well as juvenile salmonids. Forage fish are important prey for salmon, birds and other predators. Thirty-two of Vashon's 75 streams provide habitat for fish.

Walking inland also affords wildlife observation. Deer are numerous. Many Islanders say *too* plentiful a population given the deer's appetite for flowers and favorite shrubs. Their tracks are easy to spot in sand or soft soil. Raccoons are commonplace. Otters have been seen at Fisher Pond (formerly called Frenchman's Pond). At least forty species of birds use the Island's pond and freshwater wetlands (Ref. 8). Both wood ducks and hooded mergansers breed on the local ponds. Eagles look for fish and sometimes an unwary small duck (Ref. 8). The occasional ring-necked pheasant dashes across roads or screeches in the woods. Fisher Pond, a publicly accessible fresh-water pond on Vashon, is a good place for bird watching. Hawks, osprey, and ravens are increasing on the Island.

Trail walks provide sightings of many common native flora on the Island such as bracken fern, lady fern, sword fern, salal, Oregon grape, red huckleberry, evergreen huckleberry, salmonberry, snowberry, thimbleberry, bald hip rose, red-flowering currant, willow, and many varieties of moss. The common native trees are red alder, madrone, Douglas fir, Western hemlock, and big-leaf maple. Unfortunately, non-native plants, such as English ivy, holly, herb robert, and Scotch broom, are increasingly plentiful and are displacing native plants. Blackberries, of course, are ubiquitous in the Northwest as they are locally on the Island. The Himalayan and the evergreen blackberries are introduced species. However a trailing blackberry, native to the Northwest, grows along the ground, usually in disturbed sites, thickets, and dry, open forest. Its berry is prized by the Island's old timers for flavor.

III
Equipment and
Other Considerations

M ANY VASHON BEACHFRONT OWNERS do not appear to object to occasional walkers crossing their beaches at low tide. However, on beach walks, you may encounter a "no trespassing" sign. Washington State Law is quite clear that private land ownership extends to the high tide line. In some places, the State has sold tidelands to private owners. While there appears to be no definitive judicial ruling regarding the right of beach walkers to cross tidelands below the high tide mark, it is clear that beach walkers do not have a right to harvest shellfish, beachcomb, litter or disturb a private beach in the search for marine life. Beach walkers should not picnic or camp or otherwise stay on private beaches. **In summary, beach walkers should "walk lightly" without stopping on private beaches and should do so only near the water's edge at low tides to assure that they are below the high tide line and are respectful of the privacy of residents.**

Take good walking shoes. For the beaches, choose shoes that will ensure good footing on rocky, muddy, and often slippery terrain. Bring water, a lightweight rain jacket, and a sweater in any season. Breezes pick up and rain will surprise you.

Before embarking on beach walks, you must check the tide table. Time your walk so the incoming tide does not cut off your return. For the longer walks, start on the out-going tide.

It is advisable to walk with at least one other person because many parts of the beach are rocky, and often slippery due to wet coverings of eelgrass, kelp, or mud. In

Equipment and Other Considerations

some coves, walkers can sink up to their ankles. Beach walkers should also be aware of rising tides. Purchase of a tide table is strongly recommended. Tide table booklets are available at local hardware and book stores. Newspapers publish tide tables on their weather page, and the Internet is a source of tide charts.

While it is illegal to harvest shellfish on privately owned beaches, some like to harvest clams on public ones. However, beaches often are closed to harvesting due to the presence of an alga known commonly as "Red Tide," which is ingested by shellfish. It produces a biotoxin (Paralytic Shellfish Poison) that is toxic to humans. Call the "Red Tide Hotline" (1-800-562-5632) or go online to the Washington State Department of Health website (www.doh.wa.gov) to check which beaches are specifically closed to shellfish harvesting.

In the parks, there are guidelines for pets, particularly dogs. Please note the rule for each park. Common sense should be the guide for beach walks. Your pets should be under your control, to protect wildlife and others using the beaches.

IV
BEACH WALKS

THE TOTAL BEACH WALKING DISTANCE around Vashon-Maury Island has been estimated as 47 to 51 miles. The actual distance depends on the tides and on walkers' ability to shortcut the many coves by walking out on the tidelands during low tide. These beach walks should be taken in few-hour segments because of the tides. Walkers will be afforded good views of Vashon-Maury Island, Seattle, Pierce County, Mount Rainier, Tacoma, Kitsap Peninsula and the Olympic Mountains. Looking inland, walkers enjoy sights of native plants and trees along beachfront, much of which remains undeveloped. Along other stretches, walkers view interesting homes and beachfront cottages. Much of the Vashon-Maury Island shoreline has steep slopes, which are susceptible to erosion and slides. Beach walkers will encounter homes damaged by slides. Many homes have bulkheads to prevent bank erosion, but bulkheaded shorelines and other forms of beach armoring prevent waves from eroding the cliffs. The resulting sediments renew the beach. Shoreline armoring changes the beach, and therefore compromises good habitat for clams and other burrowing organisms, for eelgrass and seaweeds, for tide-zone creatures, and for egg-laying fish.

The following beach walks are described proceeding southeast from the Island's North End ferry dock and Boat Ramp Access and going clockwise around the Island.

NORTH END BOAT RAMP ACCESS TO WINGEHAVEN PARK

One-way walking distance is 1.2 miles. Allow 30 minutes.

This easy walk starts on sandy beaches, but then becomes rocky and slippery. From the dock to Dolphin

Beach Walks

Point, at extreme low tides, a sandy strip will emerge. The walk provides good views of Blake Island to the north, and the greater Seattle area and North Cascades to the east. If the tide is very low, look at the sea life under the ferry dock. Car ferry service was inaugurated from this dock in 1919 (Ref. 2).

After leaving the ferry ramp, you see homes lining the beach. This walk-in community is called Bunker Trail, after a Mr. Bunker who used to live there. Most of the homes are accessible only by trail. Many homes were once in I-5 freeway's path and moved by barge to this site in the 1960s (Ref. 7). The rocky beach is chock full of intertidal life. Look for shore crabs, moon snails, sea stars, small octopus, sea pens, sea slugs, and chitons. In late summer, seaweed covers the beach with an array of red, brown, and green algae.

The shoreline heads generally east until Dolphin Point. This beach community is also a walk-in, accessible by trail only. A famous resident of Dolphin Point was Betty MacDonald, author of *The Egg and I*. She also wrote *Onions in the Stew* about her experiences living on a trail on Vashon Island. Further on, the beach walk heads south where beautiful trees can be seen from the beach, especially in early fall. Where the beach is backed by cliffs, look for red-flowering currant in spring and mock orange in summer, both plants cascading from the cliffs. Look for a sign that marks Wingehaven Park as a Washington State Cascadia Marine Trail campsite.

ACCESS

Ample parking is available on weekends at North end ferry parking lot uphill from the ferry dock. Access the beach by going down the ramp that is east of dock and next to the restaurant.

The ramp is very slippery.

12

WINGEHAVEN PARK TO POINT HEYER (KVI BEACH)

One way walking distance is 5.9 miles. Allow 3.5 hours.

Wingehaven is a 17.7-acre shoreline-access park, known best by kayakers and beach walkers. Most of the site is a designated wetland. Wingehaven is used for hiking, bird watching, and picnicking. It is part of the Washington State Cascadia Marine Trail and may be used for overnight camping when accessed by human-powered craft. Note the remnants of an ornate bulkhead and year-round stream dressed by fragrant honeysuckle. As you walk the Island, observe where bulkheads' culverted stream outlets are too high off the beach or are constrained by piping, preventing migrating fish from entering.

This beach hike is mostly rocky if done near the high tide line, so walking it at very low tides is recommended. The beach narrows immediately past Wingehaven so watch the incoming tide if you return to Wingehaven. Wingehaven is close to Cowley's Landing, a stopping point for the Mosquito Fleet, which provided water transportation in the early 1900s (Ref. 6). Much of the way is undeveloped beach, a section of which is owned by the Muckleshoot Tribe as a place for shellfish gathering and other traditional native activities. The beach also had a brick factory and a development called Aquarium. For more information on Wingehaven Park see page 53.

Sandy beaches at Glen Acres and at Dilworth, also known as Point Beals, give respite from the slippery walking on beach rocks. Worth noting are some giant rocks probably left from the series of glaciers that occupied Puget Sound. The Rev. Dilworth held camp meetings on the beach near here.

About one mile past Point Beals, a large tidal flatland allows easy walking at low tide. Unfortunately, this area is designated a shellfish closure zone due to outflows from the Vashon wastewater treatment plant located mid Vashon. Past this cove is the site of what was

Beach Walks

Vashon Landing, another Mosquito Fleet pickup point that boomed with a mill, hotel, cannery, post office (1883) and nearby store (Ref. 9). As you walk, notice the number of bricks on the shore increases as you get near the site of the former brickyard, one of eight or nine built on the Island. Be sure to look south; occasionally Mount Rainier comes into view.

After passing the Klahanie Beach community, the next cliff-backed beach is a favorite spot for river otter. Look at the seabird nest holes. At the cliff base appears glacial till, a concrete-like mixture of sand, silt, clay, and boulders. Its making is described as the "results from being shoved, ground, and smushed by the overlying mile-thick layer of ice during the peak of the Vashon glacial advance" (Ref. 1). At high tide, the cliff's far end may require you to get wet feet. At KVI Beach, the communication tower looms. Look for a trail running close to the beach that will lead to street parking.

In clear weather, enjoy the great views of the greater Seattle area and North Cascades.

ACCESS

There is very limited parking at Wingehaven. Turn east from Vashon Hwy. SW onto Cunliffe Rd. SW, then take the first turn onto a narrow road heading downhill. Look for a sign designating Wingehaven parking. Note that there is only space for three to four cars. Take the short, steep trail down to the park surrounded by ivy-draped trees.

POINT HEYER (KVI BEACH) TO PORTAGE

One-way walking distance is 1.2 miles. Allow 30 minutes.

KVI Beach, one of the best sandy beaches on the Island, is a favorite place for Vashon youngsters to swim, picnic, and play in the sand. Note the importance of the large drift logs which add structure stabilizing the beach. At low tide, a massive sand bar curves out from the point. Killdeer nest in the beach grass.

KVI Beach is a sand spit bordering a tidal salt marsh. This salt marsh is the only one in King County that supports salicornia, a low springy vegetation foraged by many waterfowl, such as ducks and gulls. In spring and fall, sandpipers and plovers migrate past here (Ref. 8). In July, there are purple martins, and by August, swallows and martins appear in large flocks, as well as other migrating birds like grebes, loons, and sandpipers. Later in fall, gulls, terns, sparrows, and scoters return (Ref. 1). The native name for the area is *Tuqo'olil*, or "hidden spring," named after a secret spring where a young girl was hidden to keep her from unwanted marriage (Ref. 10). For more information on Point Heyer, see page 46.

On this short hike, you walk the shore of Tramp Harbor. Tramp Harbor is noted as a migrating bird stopover and for its over-wintering flock of American wigeons. The first set of pilings you pass was once a dock, a Mosquito Fleet pickup point. Later, on the shore side, pioneer Hiram Fuller built a store and a 14-room hotel. In the 1880s Chautauqua, now Ellisport, was the site of a 1200-seat pavilion (Ref. 9), the gathering spot for participants in the Chautauqua movement, an East Coast phenomenon that featured gatherings dedicated to adult education and recreation. Note the stream, Ellis Creek, culverted under Chautauqua Dr. onto the beach. The wetland across Chautauqua Dr. served as a mill pond with an adjacent lumber mill and, in later years, as a greenhouse site, a summer camp, a fuel-storage site, and a water-system reservoir. This estuary has been purchased by the County in a joint effort with the Land Trust to protect juvenile salmon.

The next pilings are Vashon Park District's Tramp Harbor Dock, a highly-used public fishing pier and base for scuba diving. Walk out on this dock for a view back to the Island and for a peek at the sea life caught by fisherfolk and divers.

The hike ends at Portage, the isthmus that links Vashon and Maury Islands. The Native Americans called this portage *StE'xugw1L*, or "where one pushes a canoe over" (Ref. 10). Here, they strung grass nets (some being 60 fathoms long) across this narrow piece of land. The Native Americans would "stir the ducks up," then, as the birds flew characteristically at low altitude between Tramp and Quartermaster Harbors, the birds got caught in the net (Ref. 11). Today, thanks to a school project, reflectors can be seen on the power lines, preventing low-flying waterfowl from colliding with the wires.

ACCESS

From Vashon Hwy. SW., turn east onto SW 204th St., which becomes Ellisport Rd. SW, until you reach the bottom of the hill; turn left onto Chautauqua Beach Dr. SW. At the corner of Chautauqua and 204th St., go right. There is a gated entrance to KVI Beach, limited parking, no ADA access, and no sanitary facilities. Do not park in private drives or block the road or mail-boxes. More parking is available further up the hill on 204th.

PORTAGE (TRAMP HARBOR) TO POINT ROBINSON PARK

One way walking distance is 3.2 miles. This walk should be done only at low tides. Fallen trees block the way at higher tides. Allow 1½–2 hours.

Portage is on the isthmus that separates Puget Sound's Tramp Harbor from Quartermaster Harbor and links Vashon and Maury Islands. The *M.V. Vashon Island*, the first of the cross-Sound auto ferries, went from Portage to Des Moines starting in 1916. The Portage store is an Island landmark, but is closed at the time of writing this booklet. It was known earlier as Van Olinda's Portage Dock Hotel Store. Across the street and overlooking the beach is a collection of rusting stationary bicycles. A public fishing pier is located 0.4 miles to the north along Dockton Rd.

Remains of an old Mosquito Fleet dock.

The Tramp Harbor beach supports large numbers of sand dollars. In the 1995–1996 survey (Ref. 3), twenty-three invertebrate species were observed, most of which were mollusks. Immediately to the east of the beach is a very steep bank, the site of many slides.

At somewhat more than a third of the way, you pass the remnants of the Fern Heath Dock, another Mosquito Fleet stop. After roughly another third of the hike are remnants of the former Maury Dock, once serving steamers which carried mail, freight, and passengers to Des Moines at the turn of the century.

ACCESS

From Vashon Hwy. SW, turn east onto 204th St. SW, which becomes SW Ellisport Rd., and follow Ellisport Rd. to Dockton Rd. SW. Turn right and follow Dockton Rd. to the intersection with Portage Way SW. There is some parking across from the Portage store, and more street parking is available along Portage Way.

The next few beach walks cover an area being reviewed for conservation by Washington State. It is the Maury

Beach Walks

Island Aquatic Reserve, which encompasses offshore waters from Luana Beach and Point Robinson, down Maury's east side to Neill Point on Vashon, and all of Quartermaster Harbor. Protected ecosystems from sea bottom to the surface include geoduck beds, eelgrass meadows, herring runs, and bottom fish.

POINT ROBINSON TO MAURY REGIONAL MARINE PARK DOCK

One-way walking distance is 1.6 miles. Allow 45 minutes.

Point Robinson Park, a 10-acre site at the east end of Maury Island, is a favorite spot to observe the J-Pod of southern Puget Sound's orca whales when it heads south to feed in Tacoma's Commencement Bay. In 1885, a fog horn was installed. Now a 1915 lighthouse overlooks a long sandy beach, which some islanders believe is the best beach on Vashon. Visitors often hear (or see with binoculars) barking sea lions on the yellow mid-channel buoy to the east. The Native Americans called this place *TsEtsa3a'p,* or "hollering across." Lushootseed linguist Vi Hilbert suggests that the word "refers to the manner in which the point of the island reaches over toward the mainland" (Ref. 10). Thanks to an agreement with the Vashon Park District, Point Robinson Park is on the Washington State Cascadia Marine Trail for overnight camping by kayakers. For more information on Point Robinson Park see page 47.

Point Robinson is a favorite area for bird watchers to see pigeon guillemots and, especially during migration, flocks of scoters and grebes. As you round Point Robinson, you see the two old Coast Guard homes built in 1908 and 1917 and the old barn built in 1887. Further on, the beach becomes rocky and is passable even at mid tides. In roughly two thirds of a mile, you cross Raecoma Beach.

Look for evidence of numerous landslides on the clayish bluffs. Vegetation on the newer slides includes pearly everlasting with its prominent white flowers. Scotch broom loves the sandy, dry, sunny location. Also watch for a gully in the cliff called by the Native Americans *Tuksiu'b*, or "where snakes landed." This gully, according to myth, is where the Snake People from the mainland slid up Maury and came out at Quartermaster Harbor to revenge a killing of a snake in the Duwamish Valley by the harbor's Native Americans (Ref. 10).

Watch out for poison oak all along Maury Island's beaches.

As you approach the undeveloped Maury Regional Park, look upward to see the long dense stand of madrones that reach to the skyline. This stand has been cited as the largest representative of the Douglas fir-Pacific Madrone/salal community in Washington State (Ref. 18). Be sure to walk to the end of the dock to look back at the madrone forest, down into the tidal life, and out to Mount Rainier. To exit at Maury Regional Park, go inland at the dock and then look for a gravel road climbing northeastward to a parking lot at the top of the hill.

ACCESS

From Vashon Hwy. SW, turn east at the junction with SW Quartermaster Dr. Then turn south onto Dockton Rd. SW and follow it to the intersection with SW Point Robinson Rd. Stay left. Follow Point Robinson Rd. to the top of the hill and then eastward till its intersection with Luana Beach Rd. Turn right and proceed to the park. Turn right and proceed to the park. There is ample parking. The upper lot provides easy access to picnic benches and a short trail providing lookouts. The lower lot provides immediate access to the trail to the lighthouse and beach. A Sani-can is available at the lower parking lot. Note "dogs on leash" sign. **Watch out for poison oak near the bank of the shoreline.**

Maury Regional Marine Park Dock to Dockton Park

One way walking distance is 5.7 miles. Allow 2.5 to 3 hours.

Maury Regional Park is an undeveloped King County Marine Park of 305 acres offering trails and excellent shoreline access. It is the site of an old gravel pit. Its sand and gravel were deposited by streams draining from the advancing glacier. The partially restored dock affords excellent views of the park and its madrone forest. The park's beach is more than one mile long. To the south is a magnificent view of the mainland and Mount Rainier.

Invertebrate species on the park's beach have been cataloged (Ref. 3). Four species of sea stars were found—mottled star, blood star, sunflower star, and purple star. Five species of crabs were found—black-clawed crab, Northern kelp crab, graceful decorator crab, Dungeness crab, and red rock crab. And five species of bivalves were noted—cockle, horse clam, sand clam, bay mussel, and jingle shell. Several types of seaweed abound in the near-shore waters. For more information on Maury Regional Marine Park, see page 42.

This walk features large undeveloped beach sections before and after the highly developed Gold Beach residential area. To traverse the Gold Beach area, walkers will need a low tide. There is no public access to the beach from the Gold Beach community.

After Gold Beach, you cross over the beachfront of the Glacier NW property, the site of a proposed large gravel mine. About one and three-quarters miles from Maury Regional Park, you see a madrone forest, not only the largest on the Island, but of a size making it notable in Puget Sound. Why is this madrone forest here? First, madrone likes porous, well-drained soils and needs sun on its broad, evergreen leaves. Second, in the first decade of the 1900s, up to 6,000 visitors a weekend came by ferry from Tacoma to Maury (Ref. 11). They camped or picnicked on the beach, and their neglected fires ran up the slopes, burning out the Douglas fir and, according to one hypothesis, allowing the madrone to dominate.

Further on, you pass the Sandy Shores community. At the south end of Maury Island, you reach the Summer-hurst area and then Piner Point. Perhaps testifying to beached drift, the Native Americans called this point *Dzuqwe'lks*, or "trash washed up on a promontory" or in a more recent translation, "smashed up, shattered promontory" (Ref. 10). This southern part of Maury Island is also known as Northilla Beach.

Following the beach west and then north along this rela-tively undeveloped stretch, you cross Manzanita Beach. In 1885, the Northwest experienced "The Chinese Riots," civil unrest during an economic depression that was marked by mobs evicting Chinese immigrants from Tacoma and Seattle. At Manzanita lived a large community of Chinese employed in fishing and salting fish. This colony, known as Hong Kong, disappeared "overnight," and the event is still a "mystery" (Ref. 11).

The distance from the Maury Regional Park dock to Manzanita Beach Rd. SW is about 3.8 miles. There is public access to Manzanita Beach via Manzanita Beach Rd., but parking space is limited. Continuing on to Dockton Park (another 1.9 miles), you pass many beach homes and the site of an old shipyard.

These southern Maury beaches are important as inter-tidal forage fish (herring and surf smelt) spawning grounds.

ACCESS

From Vashon Hwy. SW, turn east at the junction with SW Quartermaster Dr. Then turn south onto Dockton Rd. SW and follow it to the intersection with Pt. Robinson Rd. Follow SW Pt. Robinson Rd. to the intersection with 59th Ave. SW. Go right on 59th SW and then turn left onto SW 244th Street. Follow SW 244th for 0.3 miles to the parking lot. The parking lot is about a 15-minute walk from the dock.

DOCKTON PARK TO PORTAGE (QUARTERMASTER HARBOR SIDE)

One way walking distance is 3.2 miles. Allow at least 2 hours.

Dockton Park is a 23-acre King County Park known for its boat launch and moorage facilities. It offers a swimming beach, short hiking trails, picnic areas, and children's play area. Restrooms and showers are available.

The Dockton Beach is mostly mud except at higher ground. The marine life here is difficult to observe because of the muddy substrate (Ref. 3). If you walk in early spring, watch for great blue herons gathering for their annual courtship rites in inner Quartermaster Harbor. You cross Mileta Creek which upstream recently housed a heron colony of over one hundred nests. The herons seem now to scatter their nesting sites throughout the Island (Ref. 7). Soon, you need to maneuver along a dike that created Raabs Lagoon. For more information on Dockton Park, see page 34.

This hike can be very muddy in the Portage vicinity.

ACCESS

Follow Vashon Hwy. SW to SW Quartermaster Dr., turn east and follow Quartermaster Dr. until the intersection with Dockton Rd. SW. Go south (right) on Dockton Rd. to Dockton Park, 3.5 miles. There is ample parking for cars, boat and horse trailers, and motor homes. There are trails for hiking, biking, and horseback riding on the east side of Dockton Rd.

PORTAGE (QUARTERMASTER HARBOR SIDE) TO JENSEN POINT PARK

One way walking distance is 3.2 miles. Allow at least 2 hours.

The north end of Quartermaster Harbor is where the first white settlers built in November of 1877 (Ref. 2). The National Audubon Society designated Quartermaster Harbor an Important Bird Area because it is an overwintering area for Western Grebes, hosting nearly ten percent of Washington's wintering grebe population (Ref. 1).

This hike is muddy. Judd Creek is not only muddy, but very slippery. Before reaching Judd Creek, you pass what was once Quartermaster Dock, where in 1890 the steamer Sophia began service between Quartermaster and Tacoma (Ref. 2). Judd Creek, Vashon's largest, is a salmon-bearing stream. The Indian name for Judd Creek is *Sduqo'o,* or "closed in creek," a good description for its mouth's claustrophobic feel (Ref. 10).

The Burton Acres beach to the north of the Burton Peninsula has little wave action and thus has finer sand. This beach is prime habitat for Manila clams, littleneck clams, and geoducks (Ref. 3). Quartermaster Harbor is periodically closed to shellfish and seaweed harvesting because of fecal contamination. These closures have allowed more diverse and larger size clams. The Native Americans called the approximate location of the marina *DEq3o'ya*, where an "old woman gave feasts" (Ref. 10).

ACCESS

Car parking is available along SW Quartermaster Drive near its intersection with Dockton Rd.

JENSEN POINT PARK TO TAHLEQUAH FERRY TERMINAL

One way walking distance 6.3 miles. Allow at least 3 hours.

Jensen Point Park has picnic benches and a view of Quartermaster Harbor. It has a boat ramp, good for power boats, one of only a few on Vashon. The park is used year around for launching large racing sculls. A recently built boathouse holds several of these sculls. In summer, kayak lessons are available. For more information on Jensen Point Park, see page 38.

Proceeding south, you pass Camp Burton, now a meeting and convention center, known in the early 1900s as the Baptist Assembly Grounds (Ref. 9) or "Gospel Spit" (Ref.

10). Next you cross Burton Beach. After you curve south, you reach Shawnee Beach. In the late 19th century, prior to being transferred to a reservation, some of the Puyallup people would stay during the winter in long houses located at Shawnee and what is now called Governors' Row. The Native Americans called the area, *Siaba'l-qo*, or "chief's water," for a spring so fine "common people did not dare to drink here" (Ref. 10). Near here was a brick factory, one of the eight or nine once on the Island. Next you cross the mouth of Fisher Creek, an excellent example of an unarmored beach which allows salmon to migrate upstream and lets the sand build a bar protecting both the beach houses and the stream mouth (Ref. 1). The Indian name of this area is *A'lalEl*, or "old houses," once the site of an Indian village noted for extensive clam beds.

Next comes Magnolia Beach, site of the 1906 Victorian-style Marjesira Inn, now a private residence (Ref. 9). Then you cross large expanses of uninhabited beachfront. At about four miles from Jensen Point Park, you travel 1330 feet of shoreline owned by Vashon Park District and stewarded by Vashon-Maury Island Land Trust. Inland is Lost Lake, a sphagnum moss wetland and part of this conservation property. For access information, see page 40. Geoducks, eelgrass, jackknife clams, and California mussels flourish on this wide and sandy beach. Note the springs surfacing in the upper beach. This area was once called Seven Springs (Ref. 7).

The cliffs are dramatically eroding. First, wave action eats at their base. Second, the undercut glacial sediments slide onto the beach, being lubricated at their base by a platform of Lawton blue clay which settled out of quiet waters dammed by the advancing glacier. (The clay is used by Island potters.) Third, one mile of Vashon's east side is sliding outward and downward as a rotational slump block. The beach cliffs are the crumbling face of the slump block. Lost Lake is a sag pond formed in the trough along the slump's inland side. Note the clay layers

Beach Walks

on the upper beach are turned on their sides and broken, indicating a massive rotation of the area (Ref. 13).

You walk south to round Neill Point, the southern tip of Vashon. From here to the ferry dock is slippery and rocky. Note the up-ended clay layers on the beach, indicating another active geologic area. In the early 1900s, ethnographer T. T. Waterman reports this place was a Kanaka (Hawaiian) and Chinese town (Ref. 10).

To leave the beach at Tahlequah, follow a steep short trail on the east side of the ferry dock to the parking lot.

Watch for poison oak.

ACCESS

Follow Vashon Hwy. SW to SW Burton Dr. Head east on Burton Dr. to 97th Ave. SW. Go left or right and follow the road to Jensen Point Park. A toilet is available. ADA-accessible parking.

TAHLEQUAH FERRY TERMINAL TO LISABEULA PARK

One way walking distance is 6.2 miles. Allow 3.5 hours and be prepared for very muddy walking conditions.

Walk the first couple of miles at lowest tide. The beach is narrow and could be covered as the tide rises.

This beach walk provides good views of Tacoma's Point Defiance Park, Gig Harbor, and after you round Point Dalco, the Olympic Peninsula and Olympic Mountains. As the hike proceeds from Tahlequah, you pass the outlet for Tahlequah Creek. Not far from the terminal are lovely beach homes along with, from an earlier era, collapsing old cabins, perhaps fishermen's cabins. Further on, look for extensive kelp beds as the hike traverses a large expanse of uninhabited beachfront.

As the walk rounds Vashon's south end, Dalco Point, and heads north, the beach front becomes part of Spring

25

Beach Park, an undeveloped 45.8-acre park overseen by the Vashon Park District. There are no trails into this park. At the community of Spring Beach is the log-constructed former Miramar Inn. The inn, now a private residence, opened in 1906 as a holiday stop accessed by boat from Tacoma (Ref. 9). In the upcoming cliffs, look for holes which serve as bird nests.

Proceeding further, you encounter some of the nicest sand beaches on Vashon, in this case extending from Camp Sealth, originally a Camp Fire Girls camp established in 1920, to Paradise Cove. The 400-acre Camp Sealth is now owned by Camp Fire USA. The camp's waterfront is 0.8 miles long. Camp Sealth is not open to the public.

After Camp Sealth, look for a boardwalk atop the bulkhead called Bates Walk. This is another Island walk-in community. Residents park at the end of Bates Road and wheelbarrow their groceries in. The beach widens considerably to the next small point. After this point, the beach narrows and becomes rocky.

About 5.5 miles from Tahlequah, an alternate exit from the beach is available at SW Cross Landing Rd., which connects to SW Reddings Beach Rd.

Shortly before reaching Lisabeula Park, trees that have fallen from the bluffs onto the beach make this stretch difficult at high tide. You next cross a particularly muddy cove. It is best to cross this cove close to the water's edge. Christensen Creek, noted for its fish, empties into this cove, supplying its delta with sediment.

ACCESS

There is ample parking in the parking lot above the ferry terminal at Tahlequah. To access the beach, follow a steep short trail from the road on the east side of the ferry dock. **Watch for poison oak.**

LISABEULA PARK TO NORTH END FERRY DOCK AND BOAT RAMP ACCESS.

One way walking distance is 8.7 miles. Allow 5 hours.

Lisabeula, a 5.5-acre park, offers a hand-carried boat launch, a picnic area, a Sani-can, and good views of Olympic Peninsula and Olympic Mountains across Colvos Passage. Lisabeula Park is a campsite on the Washington State Cascadia Marine Trail.

Once the Lisabeula dock provided service to the Mosquito Fleet and also to Olalla across Colvos Passage. Colvos Passage is about one mile wide and 110 to 410 feet deep and separates the Island from the Kitsap Peninsula. Lisabeula was a resort with its heyday in the 1930s. Most of the old buildings were removed in the 1950s. A few cabins remained, used as a laid-back resort and housing until it was transferred to the Vashon Park District.

At times, the beach going north is narrow and exposed to waves from boats and wind. It is advisable to traverse this beach at lowest tides. The hike is very rocky at the outset, and then later becomes quite muddy. At the first cove, you will cross Green Valley Creek. Then you travel

Shinglemill Creek flows into Fern Cove Estuary.

27

a long uninhabited stretch until the Sunset Beach community. After about another ¾ mile of relatively uninhabited beach, you pass Cove, another Mosquito Fleet stop. Where the beach narrows is the former Cove Motel, first Island home to many sojourners and permanent Island residents. You need a medium tide here, and the stream mouth immediately to the north gets very muddy. After about a mile-plus, you round Peter Point, which holds a ponded wetland. This is privately owned. The Native Americans named it *Qo':ti,* or "sleeping mats" for the abundance here of cattails used in weaving (Ref. 10).

After about one and three-quarters miles from Cove, you reach the Fern Cove Sanctuary, a 13.5-acre preserve with 730 feet of Puget Sound shoreline overseen by Vashon Park District. Beach access is allowed, but to explore inland, walkers need permission from the Vashon Park District.

The wide beach is a notable estuary. You cross the source of the delta's sand which is Shinglemill Creek, named for the shingle mill operating here in 1888. It is the second largest salmon-bearing stream on the Island. Western and Least Sandpipers frequent this beach (Ref. 1). A Vashon-Maury Island Land Trust project, called the Shinglemill Creek Salmon Preserve, works to conserve the Shinglemill Watershed through acquisition, land donation, landowner education, and private conservation easements. King County Roads, Vashon Park District, and the Land Trust have more than 250 acres within the watershed under protection (Ref. 7). The 1912 Smith-Baldwin House, a King County Landmark, is next to the second creek you cross, the fish-bearing Baldwin Creek (Ref. 9).

Further on, you pass Corbin Beach. Ahead you see old pilings, the sites of Sylvan Beach and Biloxi docks, which served the Mosquito Fleet. Along this way, look for the unusual "crooked" cottage. After the last row of cabins and the end of the wide beach, you round Point Vashon,

*Sylvan Beach with Blake Island on the horizon, and the
remnants of an old Mosquito Fleet dock.*

the northernmost part of Vashon. The shore heads
toward the northeast. Look northwest to see the South-
worth Ferry landing on the Kitsap Peninsula and north to
glimpse Mount Baker.

On Point Vashon is a row of homes above the beach.
Across the water, the green island is Blake Island, a
Washington State Park. The Indian name for Blake is
Tatcu or "bull head" (Ref. 10). On the far side of Point
Vashon, you walk on a shelf that looks like rock, but is
very slippery clay. This stretch is not passable at high
tide. Watch among the cobbles for cling fish, a dark
brown fish with a suction cup on its belly. It guards its
nest among the rocks and, if disturbed, vocally chal-
lenges threats.

Once past the houses, examine the 30-foot high layers of
silt and clay exposed at the cliff base. These layers were
formed from lake sediments when glaciers dammed and
backed up water in the Puget Sound lowland (Ref. 1).
Before you leave the beach by the boat ramp (very

slippery), stop under the ferry dock to see the pilings' anemones and sea stars and admire the sandy bottom's sea pens and sea slugs.

ACCESS

Follow Vashon Hwy. SW, then turn west onto SW 216th Street. Turn left onto 111th Ave. SW and then right onto SW 220th St. Follow 220th to SW Lisabeula Rd. There is ample parking and a Sani-can.

V
TRAIL AND PARK WALKS

AGREN PARK

VASHON PARK DISTRICT RULE: *Dogs may be off-leash if not disturbing others. They are not allowed on play fields during sports seasons.*

Agren Memorial Park is a 30-acre multi-use sports park and forest conservancy located on the west side of Vashon Island off SW Bank Rd. It was donated to the community in memory of the son of the original owners, Eric and Anna Agren, who bought the property in 1917. Their son died in a WWII Japanese POW camp in 1942. The heavily wooded property has informal walking and horseback riding trails that meander through conifer stands.

A grass baseball/softball field with backstop, bleachers, parking, and Sani-cans has been developed. The field can be converted into small soccer fields during soccer season. A walking path circles the field.

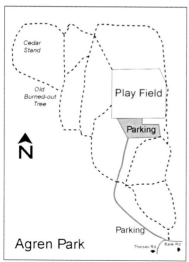

Cedar Stand

Old Burned-out Tree

Play Field

Parking

N

Parking

Agren Park

Thorsen Rd / Bank Rd

In 2004, the park underwent selective logging that decreased the density of the Douglas firs that were the main species in this park The thinning will allow salal and other undergrowth to thrive. The project included creating new trails, and connecting them with existing ones (see schematic map), including an especially enjoyable section on the west side of the park that has a stand of old cedars. Also, Earth Corps and other volunteers planted over 450 trees and ground cover including cedars, grand firs, noble firs, maples, fringe cup, Dewey's sedge, woodland strawberry, and serviceberry.

In addition, a new trail connecting Agren Park with Fisher Pond is being developed, but currently requires a walk from the exit of Agren Park east on Bank Road approximately 100 yards to the entrance to the Fisher Pond Trail. This trail entrance isn't well marked, so attention is required to enter the Fisher Pond Trail from this point (see page 35). Rights of way are being sought to complete the trail off road.

ACCESS
The entrance is at the west end of SW Bank Rd. just before the road turns left and becomes Thorsen Rd. SW. Parking is at the entrance and inside the park near the fields. ADA accessible. Sani-cans available.

BURTON ACRES PARK

VASHON PARK DISTRICT RULE: *Dogs may be off-leash if not disturbing others.*

Total distance for the outer loop is 1.15 miles and walking time is about ¾ hour.

Burton Acres Park is a 64-acre park located on the Burton Peninsula on Vashon's southeast shoreline overlooking Quartermaster Harbor. The woodland conservancy was originally acquired by King County, then deeded to the Vashon Park District in 1995.

The property conserves mature second-growth woodlands in the center portion of the peninsula. Local residents and park users have established walking, hiking, and horseback riding trails that traverse the interior between Burton and Jensen Point. Burton Camp and Conference Center is located on the southern boundary line off one of the park's central trail corridors.

This beautiful short walk is where visitors get a sense of how the Island might have looked before the first white men came to log in the 1850s. The moss-covered maples and other trees harbor licorice fern on their limbs. As in the Olympic Rain Forest, there are also several yew trees.

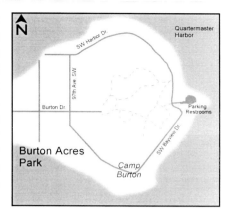

To walk the Burton Acres outer loop, look for a hiking sign across from the Jensen Point boathouse. For the longest walk, follow the outer trail, but note that there are many inner trails, and that exit trails lead to roads surrounding Burton Acres. Also a short self-guided nature trail starts at Burton Camp and Conference Center to the south of Burton Acres.

ACCESS

Follow Vashon Hwy. SW to SW Burton Dr. Head east on Burton Dr. to 97th Ave. SW. Go left or right and follow the road to Jensen Point Park. This is the best place to park. A toilet is available. ADA-accessible parking.

CHRISTENSEN POND BIRD PRESERVE

No pets or domestic animals allowed.

The 30-acre Christensen Pond Bird Preserve has been developed by the Land Trust, Vashon Audubon and King County. The loop trail can be found on Wax Orchard Road. Look for a chain across a trail and a Land Trust Nature Preserve sign. The trail leads, after a couple of hundred feet, to a juncture marked by a memorial plaque remembering four young Vashon environmentalists (Sarah Hodnett Hacker, Richard Hacker, Susan Skinner Konecki and John Konecki) who died in an airplane accident. The loop trail is about .6 miles long. Pond access is limited by heavy vegetation but a good viewing site can be found near the north side. The pond is primarily visited by ducks. A spur trail from 240th Street is about .15 miles from the loop trail and intersects the pond trail about .2 miles from the juncture.

ACCESS

Coming from the north, follow Vashon Hwy to SW 204th St., turn west, then go south on 111th Avenue, then west on 220th St., then south on Wax Orchard Road for 1.2 miles. Coming from the south, turn off onto Wax Orchard Road at the intersection with the Highway. The main trailhead is about 2 miles from this highway intersection. The only parking spaces are the road shoulders on Wax Orchard or 240th.

DOCKTON PARK

Dogs must be on a leash.

Dockton Park is a 23-acre shoreline activity park located on Maury Island off Dockton Rd. SW overlooking Quartermaster Harbor. It is owned and administered by King County.

In 1892, a large floating dry dock was built at Dockton, the site of a booming industry that built boats, including ocean-going vessels. There was a huge old building in Dockton, recently torn down, that was a boarding house for the workers. A hotel soon followed, but is long gone. In the early 1900s, passenger fare from Tacoma to Dockton by steamer was 25 cents. The row of charming high-bank homes on the south side of the harbor belonged to the managers of the boat works and was called "piano row" because the owners had the money to own pianos.

Available are a boat launch ramp and floating dock for both motorized and hand-carried craft, ample parking, temporary moorage slips, and a marina facility with piers, concrete walkways, and an administrative office. The shoreline has a roped-off swimming beach, grassy and sandy play areas, a playground, picnic tables, and a bathhouse with restrooms. A picnic shelter is currently being rebuilt with plans to finish construction by summer 2007.

The wooded upland portions extend across Dockton Road to access walking, equestrian, and biking trails linking portions of the park with adjacent King County land parcels (Dockton Forest Leased Site, now called Maury Island Forest, see page 41). Some of these trails cross private property, and boundaries with private property, King County lands, and park land are not always clear.

Access

Follow Vashon Hwy. SW to SW Quartermaster Dr., turn east and follow Quartermaster Dr. until the intersection with Dockton Rd. SW. Go south (right) on Dockton Rd. until you reach Dockton Park, 3.5 miles. Parking is ample for cars, boat and horse trailers, and motor homes. There are trails for hiking, biking, and horseback riding on the east side of Dockton Rd., but be aware there may be unmarked boundaries with private land.

Fisher Pond

No pets or domestic animals allowed.

Fisher Pond is a 90-acre freshwater and terrestrial conservancy located west of Vashon Town on SW Bank Rd. and close to Agren Park. It is the headwaters of the 255-acre Shinglemill Creek Salmon Preserve. Shinglemill Creek has juvenile coho and cutthroat all the way south to Cove Road. Adult fish go into the stream only at spawning and run as far as the Vashon Airport.

Islander Bill Fisher purchased the Fisher Pond's east acreage in 1966. He cared for the property as a wildlife refuge and purchased further acreage in 1970, 1975, and 1978 to complete what is now Fisher Pond Park. He continued to steward the pond and wetland areas until his death in 2002.

Bill Fisher donated Fisher Pond and its adjacent woods to the Island community in 1998 by giving the property to the Vashon-Maury Island Land Trust. In turn, the Land Trust and Vashon Park District partnered to secure

Fisher Pond

a $1.25 million grant from the Washington State Inter-agency Committee for Outdoor Recreation. This grant, known now as the Fisher Fund, has acquired more conservation properties within Shinglemill Creek's upper watershed. The Shinglemill Salmon Preserve is a Land Trust project that partners with the Vashon Park District, Friends of Fern Cove, private landowners, and King County.

The site contains shallow Fisher Pond (formerly known as Frenchman's Pond), a quaking aspen grove in the southeast corner, and is heavily wooded. Previous uses, in addition to logging over the years, included vegetable gardens, grazing fields, greenhouses, and a mink farm west of the pond where the Fisher caretaker residence and building stands.

Fisher Pond offers opportunities for bird watching (particularly wood ducks), nature study, and ice-skating when weather allows. On occasion, otters have come up Shinglemill Creek from Colvos Passage and have been seen at Fisher Pond.

Public access is permitted on the trail that enters the property from the pond's southeast edge on SW Bank Rd. The forested trail leads to a picnic area on the pond's northwest corner. Access is not allowed in the area where the Fisher caretaker's building is located. The trail around Fisher Pond is about 2/3 of a mile long. Due to the fact that this is a conservancy rather than a park, no ADA facilities or entrances have been developed, although wheelchairs are allowed on the trail.

A new trail has been established by the Vashon-Maury Island Land Trust that runs contiguous with the northern section of the Fisher Pond Trail from Cove Road almost to Agren Park. A junction is about 240 feet from the Fisher Pond Trail entrance. Turning left (west) the trail is contiguous with the old Fisher Pond Trail (past the picnic site), and continues west toward Agren Park (follow the signs). The trail crosses a private road, and continues to Bank Road, along which a walker must travel about 100 yards to the entrance of Agren Park.

Turning right at the junction the new trail first crosses an old apple orchard cleared of blackberries and re-planted by Land Trust volunteers. After half a mile, it crosses 115th Street and continues 100 feet north on the east side of the road. Soon you will see a small pond and a field of trees planted by Boy Scout Troop 294 in March 2006. After passing through cedar, fir, and other forest stands, the trail ends at Cove Road.

Under the terms of Bill Fisher's gift, public usage is allowed with the following restrictions: **no domestic animals (leashed or unleashed)** on the property in order to protect the site's wildlife, wetlands, and water quality; no motorized vehicles; no wheeled vehicles except for baby carriages or wheelchairs; no hunting; fishing only according to applicable laws and with barbless hooks; no fires and no camping.

Trails: From the Bank Rd. access in the southeast corner to the picnic area in the northwest corner, or to Agren Park, or to Cove Road.

Trail and Park Walks

ACCESS

From Vashon Hwy. SW, follow SW Bank Rd. west for
1.1 mile. Near the hill's bottom, a cabled-off trail starts
at the southeast corner of Fisher Pond. The trail is
blocked to vehicles, which must park along Bank Rd.

INSPIRATION POINT

VASHON PARK DISTRICT RULE: *Dogs may be off-leash if not
disturbing others.*

Inspiration Point is a 0.9-acre viewpoint located on the
east shoreline of Vashon Island off Vashon Hwy. SW
overlooking outer Quartermaster Harbor. A small turnout
with a limited number of parking spaces and a picnic site
provide scenic views of Quartermaster Harbor, Puget
Sound's East Passage, and Mount Rainier.

The area was cleared in the 1930s to make a lookout.
The Chamber of Commerce acquired the small plot
around 1935 and later gave it to the park district. The
millstone, origin unknown, was placed there after WWII
(Ref. 19).

ACCESS

On Vashon Hwy. SW between Pillsbury Rd. SW and SW
266th Lane. Turn east into the parking area. ADA
accessible.

JENSEN POINT PARK

VASHON PARK DISTRICT RULE: *Dogs may be off-leash if not
disturbing others.*

Jensen Point Park is a 4.0-acre shoreline activity park
located on the east shore of Burton Peninsula. The property was originally acquired by King County as part of
Burton Acres Park, then deeded in 1995 to, and developed by, the Vashon Park District. An archeological dig
at a shell midden on Jensen Point in 1996 demonstrates
that the tribes used the site extensively for fish processing
and summer camp as long ago as 1000 years (Ref. 15).
Native-American Lucy Gerand and her partner Tom lived

on a houseboat at Jensen Point and harvested shellfish till the late 1920s. Other S'Homamish were born and raised on Vashon in the 20s and 30s. Many moved later to Puyllaup. The archeological site was excavated by the Burke Museum in cooperation with the Puyallup Tribe of Indians and Vashon School District.

Although the area has been used for personal food sources, King County has now placed Quartermaster Harbor off-limits to shellfish harvesting, due to the frequent presence of "red tide" shellfish toxin. (See page 10 for information on shellfish harvesting.)

The site provides access to Quartermaster Harbor for both motorized and hand-carried crafts. There is ample parking for cars and boat trailers. Jensen Point and Dockton Parks, and a small, short ramp beside the Northend ferry dock, are the Island's only public motorized-boat launches. There is a small grassy area with picnic tables along the sand and cobblestone beach.

A boathouse stores kayaks, canoes and rowing shells for the district's rowing program, in cooperation with the local rowing club. Kayak and rowing classes are available for all ages. During the summer, a concessionaire rents kayaks and gives instruction.

ACCESS

Follow Vashon Hwy. SW to SW Burton Dr. Head east on Burton Dr. to 97th Ave. SW. Go left or right and follow the road to Jensen Point Park. A toilet is available. ADA-accessible parking.

LISABEULA PARK

VASHON PARK DISTRICT RULE: *Dogs may be off-leash if not disturbing others.*

Lisabeula Park is a 5.5-acre shoreline park located on the west side of Vashon overlooking Colvos Passage at the end of SW 220th St. The east end of the property conserves a wooded ravine and hillside. The shoreline area has been improved with a grassy play area, picnic tables, a hand-carried boat launch, and a designated primitive campsite for the Washington State Cascadia Marine Trail. The winding road is owned and maintained by King County.

The site is located directly north of Christensen Cove, a sensitive estuary that supports eelgrass.The stream and cove were named after Captain Lars Christensen, the builder, owner, and operator of the Virginia boats in the Mosquito Fleet, who lived there.

Lisabeula was once a beach resort with its heyday in the 1930s. It included a dance hall, general store, and cabins as well as a boat works. Some cabins remained as a laid-back resort and housing until it became a park.

ACCESS

From Vashon Hwy. SW, take SW 204th St. west to 111th Ave. SW following the road left; then go right on SW 220th St. Follow 220th to SW Lisabeula Rd. which drops down to the waterfront. There is ample parking and a Sani-can.

LOST LAKE

No pets or domestic animals allowed.

Lost Lake is 38-acres of shoreline, woods, and sphagnum-bearing wetland located on the eastern shore of Vashon overlooking Quartermaster Harbor and south of Inspiration Point and opposite Maury's Manzanita Beach. At the request of the Island Land Trust, King County transferred the land to Vashon Park District in 1995. Lost Lake was dubbed "Lizard Lake" by old-timers because it is inhabited by abundant rough-skinned newts. The Land Trust stewards the property as eelgrass shoreline and rare sphagnum wetland which supports Labrador tea. The property is habitat for eagles, Cooper's hawks, red-tailed hawks, great horned owls, and herons. The shoreline is habitat for geoducks, jackknife clams, and California mussels. It contains spawning beds for surf smelt and pacific herring.

ACCESS

There are no trails inland from the beach and no formal access to the beach, wetland and woods from the inland side. Boaters may access the shoreline. The Island's horse-riders maintain trails (some of which are over private land) through the Lost Lake area as part of a prime trail-riding circuit which traverses private property. To protect the sensitive wetland, permission for use by large groups or for research is given by the Vashon-Maury Island Land Trust.

MARJORIE STANLEY FOREST

Horses and dogs allowed.

This 17-acre parcel was purchased by the Stanley family in 1910 and later donated to the State and is now owned by King County. This is a relatively undeveloped park with several trails, but they are not well maintained or signed, and some run into private property. Part of the property is adjacent to woodlands donated by the Stanley family to the Vashon Veterans of Foreign Wars.

ACCESS

To reach an entry trail go north .2 miles on Vashon Highway from its junction with Quartermaster Drive. Look for a Marjorie Stanley Wildlife and Wilderness Area sign or two yellow posts. The trails may be reached from either of two entrances on the Highway.

MAURY ISLAND FOREST

Horses and dogs allowed.

This mixed forest, undeveloped 60-acre site (also referred to as the Dockton Forest Leased Site) was transferred to King County from the State. It is a maze of trails, often poorly marked or not evident, many used by mountain bikers. The trails will likely be improved in time by Vashon equestrians.

Trail and Park Walks

Twenty acres of this site can be accessed from Dockton Road (roughly a half mile from the King County Dockton Park) or the north side of 260th. Both this 20 acres and the 40-acre site can be accessed from trails on the south side of 260th Street. There are no signs. The trails may run into private land. Parking is only available on the shoulder of the roads.

MAURY REGIONAL MARINE PARK

Dogs must be on a leash.

Total hike distance is about 3 miles. Allow 1½ hours.

Maury Island Regional Marine Park is an undeveloped 305-acre King County shoreline activity park and conservancy. Trails and shoreline access development has been postponed. The park includes portions of a former sand-and-gravel pit operation, including its access roadways and waterfront loading piers and numerous unmarked trails. Plans include a primitive campsite for the Washington State Cascadia Marine Trail.

The dock has been partially restored for fishing and temporary moorage. Portions of the upland madrone woodland may be developed to provide grassy play areas, picnic facilities, and other day-use activities. An ADA-accessible Sani-can is available near the dock.

From the park and its dock are excellent views of Mount Rainier, Puget Sound's East Passage and Tacoma's Commencement Bay, and a vista from Federal Way to Tacoma. The park and dock are accessed by a gravel roadway (blocked to public vehicle access) from the parking lot. The park is lightly used by walkers and equestrians. There are no picnic tables at the beach, but driftwood logs provide quiet spots for sitting and enjoying the scenery. For walking the off-road trails, good traction shoes are strongly advised.

Multiple fires in 1915, the 30s and the 50s, as well as the south-southeasterly exposure, resulted in vegetation

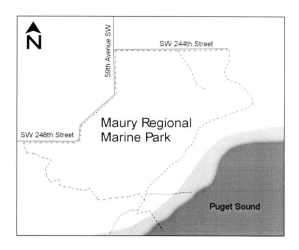

which is not always typical of the of the area. And because it is in the "rain-shadow" of the island, it is not unusual for it to receive 25-30 inches of rainfall when Vashon's northwest side receives 47 inches. The park is dominated by a madrone grove that thrives in the low rainfall, sandy, well-drained soils, and southeastern exposure. This madrone-Douglas fir plant community is listed as a Priority 1 ecosystem for protection in the 1995 *State of Washington Natural Heritage Plan* due to its rarity, threats and lack of protection. As well as the madrones, there are numerous alders, big leaf maples, and Douglas firs. The bluffs have filberts, honeysuckle, poison oak and manroot (or wild cucumber). On the beach there's artemisia.

On foot, follow the gravel road from the parking lot down to the dock. Watch for great views of Mount Rainier on clear days. At 0.4 mile, a trail will go off to the right. Avoid this trail; in the past it was posted with a rock slide warning sign. Proceed downhill to the dock, at about 0.6 mile, which was recently partially rebuilt by King County. At the end of the dock, observe eelgrass in the clear water and mussels and sea stars on the pilings. The pilings are a favored place for cormorants and gulls. For a good view of the madrone forest, look back at Maury Island. To the southwest is the community of Gold Beach.

A couple of short trails can be followed. One heads east (the trailhead is near the sani-can) and ends at the shoreline after 800 feet. Another trail heads west on the plateau just above the beach and ends at a makeshift bench overlooking the shoreline after a tenth of a mile.

Walkers can return to the parking area or can do a loop trail by following the path back to the plateau just above the beach area. Look for a white pole festooned with chain links and follow a narrow trail uphill. The climb will gain about 470 feet of elevation. At 1.1 miles (from the parking lot), there will be a junction with a trail coming from the right. Stay left and proceed upwards. Straight ahead is a very steep sandy hillside. Hikers, particularly children, should avoid going off trail and getting too close to this area since it is a slide zone. By staying on the path, you will soon be on a sandy trail that climbs steeply toward the road. On this trail are several good spots to pause and look at the vistas and observe freighters moving slowly to or from the Port of Tacoma. At the top of the trail, a juncture is reached with a trail to the left, which offers a view of the gravel mining operation under lease arrangements with the King County Park District. Stay to the right and then at the road (SW 248th), turn right. Around the bend, near the Swallow's Nest Bed & Breakfast, good views will again be available of Mount Rainier and the surrounding area. Follow the road to 59th SW and then turn right on SW 244th to get back to the parking lot. A short trail of sorts can be followed off SW 244th, which proceeds for about 0.1 mile but affords no views.

ACCESS

Follow Vashon Hwy. SW to SW Quartermaster Dr., turn east and follow Quartermaster Dr. until the inter-section with Dockton Rd. SW. Go south (right) on Dockton Rd. for 0.6 miles until the intersection with SW Point Robinson Rd. Stay left and then follow Point

Robinson Rd. for 1.4 miles to the intersection with 59th Ave. SW. Turn right on 59th to SW 244th and then turn left. Follow SW 244th for 0.3 miles to the parking lot.

OBER PARK

VASHON PARK DISTRICT RULE: *Dogs must be on a leash at all times and are not allowed in the playground area.*

Ober Park is a 5.5-acre multi-use community park located in the center of Vashon Island on the north end of Vashon Town on Vashon Hwy. SW. The park also includes the Vashon Branch of the King County Library. King County leases the library property from the Vashon Park District.

Ober Activity Center is located in the center of the site. The building contains a springboard-mounted floor performance space for gymnastics, dance classes, theater, movies and concerts; a craft/meeting room; and the administrative offices of the Vashon Park District.

The partially wooded site has picnic tables and a beautiful children's playground. The grassy lawns are used for summer gatherings, community festivals, and concerts.

ACCESS

Parking is at the Ober Activity Center/Vashon Park District Office, 17130 Vashon Hwy. SW. ADA accessible.

PARADISE RIDGE

Dogs must be on a leash at all times.

Total walk distance is about 1.1 mile around the loop trail. Allow about 25 minutes.

Paradise Ridge Park is a 43-acre park developed as an equestrian park that has become a multi-use and large-event center. It is located in the center of Vashon Island off SW 220th St. The former Nike missile site was conveyed as surplus property to King County, then to the Vashon Park District when the district was established in 1989. Portions of the site conserve stands of second-growth woodlands. A cross-country equestrian jumping

Trail and Park Walks

course has been cleared around the perimeter of the site and is also used for hiking, cross-country track competition and practice, and horseback and mountain bike riding. Groups associated with events may camp within the park. The central portion of the property has been developed into an equestrian center with training and showing rings, two judging booths,

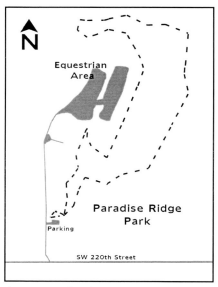

arenas, outdoor stalls, and a caretaker's house.

A group picnic area and a basketball court are located in a wooded area in the southern portion of the site adjacent to the main entry. The Paradise Ridge Stewardship and User Group in conjunction with Vashon Park District developed a Site Management Plan, which proposes to develop dedicated walking and biking trails, picnic areas, and an arboretum.

ACCESS

Follow Vashon Hwy. SW to SW 204th St. (from the North) or SW 216th St. (from the South). Go to 111th Ave. SW, go south, follow the curve onto SW 220th St. The park entrance is on SW 220th St. between Old Mill Rd. SW and 111th Ave. SW. ADA accessible. Sani-cans are available.

POINT HEYER (KVI BEACH)

Dogs may be off-leash if not disturbing others.

Point Heyer (KVI Beach) is a 13.5-acre privately owned property located on Point Heyer on the east shoreline of Vashon. A radio antenna is in the middle of the property on the sandy shoreline. Although hiking and shoreline enthusiasts have developed a series of walking trails along the sandy beach and through the marine and estuarine habitat areas, naturalists urge visitors to stay out of the salt marsh, where fragile invertebrates, a special community of salt-tolerant plants, and many species of nesting and migrating birds are sensitive to disturbance. The line of posts demarcate the area that should be viewed but not entered. This salt marsh is the only one in King County that supports salicornia, a low vegetation foraged by many waterfowl, such as ducks and gulls. The beach offers sunbathing, picnicking and wildlife viewing.

Trails: From the trailhead on SW 204th St., a short walk leads to the beach.

ACCESS

From Vashon Hwy. SW., turn east onto SW 204th St., which becomes Ellisport Rd. SW, until you reach the bottom of the hill; turn left onto Chautauqua Beach Dr. SW. At the corner of Chautauqua and 204th St., go right. There is a gated entrance to KVI Beach, limited parking, no ADA access, and no sanitary facilities. Do not park in private drives or block the road or mailboxes. More parking is available further up the hill on 204th.

POINT ROBINSON PARK

VASHON PARK DISTRICT RULE: *Dogs may be off-leash if not disturbing others.*

Point Robinson Park is a 10-acre shoreline park and historical and marine conservancy located on the eastern point of Maury Island off SW Point Robinson Rd. overlooking Puget Sound's East Passage. It was named in honor of one of the Wilkes Expedition's crew members, John Robinson.The site has provided fog and lighthouse services for vessels since 1885, when the first lighthouse keeper's dwelling was built. The present lighthouse was built in 1915 and has a fifth-order Fresnel lens, but has been automated since 1978. It is on the State Register of Historic Places. Although there is often someone at the lighthouse on Sundays around noon, tours of the lighthouse should be arranged by calling the Keepers of Point Robinson Lighthouse at 206-463-0920. The Vashon Park District owns the upland part of the park; the remainder is on long-term lease from the US Coast Guard.

The property conserves an extensive sandy beach shoreline, a saltwater marsh, and upland woodlands. On the upland area are walking trails and a few picnic tables. This park is a favorite for sunbathing and beachcombing and is a good spot to observe orca whales when they are near the Island, in particular J-Pod when it heads south to feed in Tacoma's Commencement Bay. Visitors can often hear (or see with binoculars) barking sea lions on the yellow mid-channel buoy to the east. Point Robinson is also an excellent area for bird watching, especially pigeon guillemots and overwintering flocks of scoters and grebes. As well, migrating flocks of songbirds, such as western tanagers, may be seen in the trees along the hillside before crossing the water north. Steller's jays and yellow-rumped (Audubon's) warblers also appear here.

In 1998, the Friends of Point Robinson Stewardship Group was formed and proposes to enhance the site's ecology, develop interpretation opportunities, rehabilitate the historic buildings (two officers' residences built in 1908 and 1917, a garage, and a barn built in 1887), provide adequate parking, and create trails. By an arrangement between Vashon Park District and Washington State Cascadia Marine Trail, Point Robinson Park is available for overnight camping by kayakers.

In 2003, the Vashon Park District completed renovations on the Captain's Quarters and it is now available for weekly rental. It is completely furnished and sleeps six (no pets). It may be viewed on the district's web-site at www.vashonparkdistrict.org, and reservations made by calling the park district's office at (206) 463-9602.

Trails: There is limited walking in the park itself. The upper part of the park has a short trail accessible from the parking lot. This trail leads to picnic tables and lookout points for views of the Sound. The lower parking lot provides immediate access to the trail to the lighthouse and beach. A trail at the east side of the upper park leads to the lower park. The beach is accessible during all but high tides.

ACCESS

Follow Vashon Hwy. SW to SW Quartermaster Dr., turn east and follow Quartermaster Dr. until the intersection with Dockton Rd. SW. Go south (right) on Dockton Rd. for 0.6 miles until the intersection with SW Point Robinson Rd. Stay left. Follow Point Robinson Rd. to its end. There are parking and picnic facilities in the upland area. To access the lighthouse and beach more directly, drive past the upland parking and go downhill to more parking. There is no access to the historic buildings at this time, with the exception of the Captain's Quarters which may be rented by the week, as noted above, and the Lighthouse if there is someone there on Sunday or by appointment. Park is ADA accessible and has Sani-cans available.

SHINGLEMILL SALMON PRESERVE

No pets or domestic animals allowed.

This 244-acre site is owned by the Land Trust. This preserve serves primarily to protect the Shinglemill Creek, an important salmon stream. There is limited walking available along an old road now serving as the trail. The trail offers good views of Shinglemill Creek, particularly from the bridge, moss covered trees, old logging stumps and ends after less than half a mile at a clearing. The Land Trust has done extensive replanting in the site. Much of the surrounding area is watershed and the trail can be very muddy in winter. This is sensitive habitat and visitors should not walk in the marsh or creek. The walk is an in-out trail about ½ mile long.

ACCESS

Trail and Park Walks

Coming from the north, turn west onto Cedarhurst Road. Follow the main road for 1.3 miles to the trailhead. The trailhead has no sign, but a green metal gate leads to an old logging road which is the trail. (Also look for the Fern Cove Nature Preserve sign which is just .1 miles north of the trailhead.) From the south, the trailhead is 1.4 miles from the intersection of 148th Street and Westside Highway.

SPRING BEACH PARK

No pets or domestic animals allowed.

Spring Beach Park is a 45.8-acre shoreline park and marine, freshwater, and terrestrial conservancy located on Colvos Passage on the southwest shore of Vashon south of Spring Beach community. The site is accessible from the waterfront and is designated a primitive campsite area for the Washington State Cascadia Marine Trail. At the present time, the steep site has no roadway access.

ACCESS
Water access only. No land access. No ADA facilities.

VASHON ISLAND CENTER FOREST

Pets and domestic animals allowed. Dogs may be off-leash if not disturbing others. Watch for signage that may prohibit dogs from certain sensitive areas (such as wetlands).

The loop hikes described below vary from about 2.5 to 3.6 miles. Walking distances are variable. Allow 2.5 hours

King County manages two large parcels on Vashon-Maury Island. The larger parcel of 200 acres is somewhat north of the center of Vashon Island. About 160 acres are recently planted forest. Adjacent to this property to the west and north is an 80-acre landfill site owned by the Solid Waste Division of the King County Department of Natural Resources and Parks. To the northeast are 70 acres recently acquired by the Land Trust. The north

---

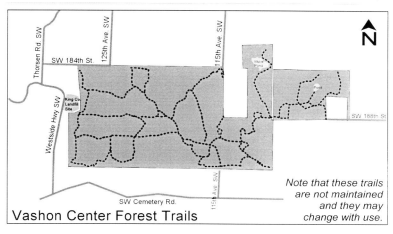

Vashon Center Forest Trails

Note that these trails are not maintained and they may change with use.

parcel (owned by the Land Trust) holds Mukai Pond, which is seasonal. The northeast parcel holds Meadowlake Pond.

This site offers the Island's most extended forest walk and gives you a sense of almost being in the wild. The areas have long been used by the Vashon community as hiking, equestrian and bicycle trails. Hikers should note that boundaries with privately held parcels are often not well marked.

This 350-acre site is an important area on the Island, serving as a major open space recharge area for the Island's aquifer. There is seasonal drainage that flows generally south and ultimately into Judd Creek (Ref. 5).

Vegetation is typical of the Island: salal, Oregon grape, blackberry, red elderberry, thimbleberry, honeysuckle, ferns, and invasive species like Scotch broom, ivy, and holly trees, particularly along edges of recent logging or at the borders of the landfill area. Madrone, big leaf maple, red alder, Douglas fir, hemlock, and western red cedar are the dominant trees.

The Island Center Forest offers about 9.5 miles of trails

Trail and Park Walks

(Ref. 5). Note that getting lost is easy in these 350 acres and so carrying a compass is advised, especially on overcast days when hikers cannot get their bearings from the sun.

There are multiple trails, many of which are maintained by the equestrians; but there are no signs, and some trails just end at private property lines. For the longest walk, about two hours, head north on 115th SW from SW Cemetery Rd, then turn right at the second trail and head east. Look for large Douglas fir trees. Take the north-heading trail at the first junction; otherwise you end up at a wire fence marking private property along the east boundary of the Forest. Trails lead north and west from this point. Taking west-heading trails will lead to the King County Solid Waste Transfer Site—known to Islanders as the "dump." (Going east along any of several central trails will eventually lead to private land.)

In the center of the Forest, in fall through early spring or after rainfalls, expect to encounter muddy spots and occasional pools of water. Some of this part of the Forest has been clear-cut in the recent past. The western terminus of the two east-west trails is a trail that runs roughly north-south and is bounded on its west by a wire fence marking the dump. Hikers can follow this trail northward to SW 184th St. To return to the parking area at the cemetery, follow the trail south and then east. Follow the main trail to a dirt roadway, which comes out on SW Cemetery Rd. (Other south-heading trails lead to Cemetery Rd., but pass through private property.)

For shorter walks, start on 115th SW at the cemetery on SW Cemetery Rd. and follow the 115th SW northward, then follow the trail as it turns west. Then take a shorter or longer loop (see map) to return to parking area.

ACCESS

Follow Vashon Hwy. SW to SW Cemetery Rd. The best place to park is on Cemetery Rd. at 115th Ave. SW. Trails are also accessible from the northwest at SW 184th St.

Any entry from the east would require permission from private landowners and is discouraged.

THE VILLAGE GREEN

Dogs must be on a leash at all times.

The Village Green Park is a 15,600 square foot pocket park in the Vashon town center. It is located on the west side of Vashon Highway just north of the intersection of Bank Road and Vashon Highway. The property was purchased by the Vashon Island Growers' Association (VIGA) in 1999 with the help of the Vashon community and then given to the Vashon Park District. VIGA had been using the site for a Saturday market for Island farmers, as well as for Island craftspeople to sell their wares. There are picnic tables and it continues to host the Saturday market, featuring home-grown and organic produce every Saturday from April through October.

ACCESS

There is no parking at the Green site except for ADA spaces. Parking is available on week-ends near the bank, on the street, and in the grocery store parking lot.

WINGEHAVEN PARK

VASHON PARK DISTRICT RULE: *Dogs may be off-leash if not disturbing others.*

Wingehaven is a 17.7-acre shoreline access park, known best by kayakers and beach walkers. The land was purchased in 1914 from Mary Dysert by Captain William Cowley, who provided dock space for the Mosquito Fleet, including the Virginia V. He began a speculative development named Twyckenham Estates, establishing an elaborate Italian garden with ponds, topiary, statuary (some remnants still decorate the seawall), exotic trees, and shrubs. The Estates failed during the Depression; no lots were sold or buildings built. Two other people owned it before it was acquired in 1950 by Carl Winge, a retired shipbuilder. He named it Wingehaven, and restored one of

Trail and Park Walks

the ponds, remodeled the house, and constructed a tennis court. The Winge family sold most of the property to King County in 1969, retaining a small parcel on the SE border for a house. The property was transferred to Vashon Park District in 1995.

The Wingehaven Park Stewardship Group developed and administers a Site Management Plan. Most of the site is a designated wetland. The main uses are hiking, bird watching, and picnicking. It is part of the Washington State Cascadia Marine Trail available for overnight human-powered craft camping.

ACCESS

There is very limited parking at Wingehaven. From Vashon Hwy. SW, turn east on Cunliffe Rd. SW, then take the first turn onto a narrow road heading downhill. Look for a sign designating Wingehaven parking. Note that there is only space for three to four cars. There is a short, steep trail down to the park. A Sani-can is available. There are no ADA facilities.

VI
MIXED TRAIL AND STREET WALKS

BURTON ACRES AND PENINSULA

This is about a two-mile walk, and is extended by a stroll through the Burton Acres Park (see description on page 32).

Start at the Burton store, Harbor Mercantile, at the flashing light in Burton. Walk east up SW Burton Dr., turn left on 97th Ave. SW and walk around the Burton Peninsula, returning to the Burton store. The road is wooded, and there are numerous houses sited mainly on the water side. The southern corner of the peninsula is also the site of the Burton Camp and Conference Center.

ACCESS

Parking may be found across from the Burton store, at the corner of Vashon Hwy. SW and SW Burton Dr.

DOCKTON/MAURY ISLAND LOOP

Total distance: 2.2 miles. Allow about an hour.

This walk is principally on Dockton Park property and the recently-designated, 60-acre Maury Island Forest (see page 41). However, the trail may run through private land.

The Dockton hiking trail starts at the parking lot on Dockton Rd. SW across from Dockton Park. Look for an equestrian sign. Follow the trail east to the border of the Glacier Northwest property, then follow the loop trail back to the main trail and return to the parking lot.

ACCESS

Follow Vashon Hwy. SW to SW Quartermaster Dr., turn east and follow Quartermaster Dr. to the intersection with Dockton Rd. SW. Go south (right) on Dockton Rd.

until you reach Dockton Park, 3.5 miles. The parking lot is across from Dockton Park. Restrooms and picnic areas are across the road at Dockton Park.

Loop Walk to Maury Regional Marine Park

Approximate distance: Six miles. Allow 3 hours. Elevation gain: About 900'.

Park on 75th Ave. SW and Dockton Rd. SW at the KING 5 towers (this stretch of 75th is known locally as Pig Lane for a former small pig farm). Walk south to SW 240th, turn left uphill to SW Pt. Robinson Rd. Continue on Pt. Robinson Rd., noting the former chicken farm near the top of the hill, and turn right at 59th Ave SW. Turn left onto SW 244th St. and walk 0.3 mi. to Maury Regional Park parking lot. Follow the gravel road from the parking lot down to the dock. Watch for great views of Mount Rainier on clear days. At 0.4 miles, a trail will go off to the right. Avoid this trail; it is posted with a rock slide warning sign. Proceed downhill to the dock, at about 0.6 mile, which was recently partially rebuilt by King County. At the end of the dock, visitors can observe eelgrass in the clear water, and mussels and sea stars clinging underwater on the pilings. The pilings are a favored place for cormorants and gulls. A good view of the madrone forest can be seen by looking back at Maury Island. To the southwest is the community of Gold Beach. (Please turn to page 42 for a description of Maury Regional Marine Park.)

Walkers can return to the parking area or do a loop trail by following the path back to the plateau just above the beach area. Look for a white pole festooned with chain links. Follow a narrow trail uphill. The climb gains about 470 feet of elevation. After 1.1 miles from the parking area, there will be a junction with a trail coming from the right. Stay left and proceed upwards. Straight ahead is a very steep sandy hillside. Hikers, and particularly children, should avoid going off trail and getting too close to this slide-zone area. By staying left on the path, hikers will soon be on a sandy trail that climbs steeply toward the road. On this trail are several good spots to pause and look at the vistas and observe freighters slowly moving toward or from the Port of Tacoma. Near the top, stay right (the trail heading left goes to an overlook at the gravel pit). At the road, turn left and walk down SW 248th St. Follow 248th to 75th Ave. SW and turn right. The Vashon Island Golf and Country Club is on the left. Follow 75th back to the start.

VII
STREET WALKS

ORIGINALLY, MOST OF THE INTERIOR of the Island was heavily forested. These woods were clear-cut during the late 1800s, but have returned as second growth, and perhaps third growth in some areas. The settlers cleared land for communities and farms, which were usually close to the water. Often no roads linked the different shoreline communities. After the logging, the "roads" cleared by loggers and the horse trails that grew up to connect communities eventually became many of the roads we have today. When walking around the Island on these roads, one often goes through second growth forests and passes the sites of old homesteads long gone. There are now homes, farms and pastures, two small airports, orchards, parks, and schools.

The Island was formed by, and subjected to, the forces of glacial activity, the last being some 15,000 years ago. The glaciers moved south, pushing their collection of rocks, grinding and pulverizing them, then receded north. When one walks north to south on Vashon, one is usually on a ridge top with not too much up and down. When walking east to west, one constantly descends into or climbs out of the valleys gouged by the glaciers. Streams have done their own work, eroding some impressive valleys in other orientations.

The walks below cover some of the early "roads," walked today by a group of people who like to travel the Island on foot.

BURMA ROAD LOOP

Total distance: 2.9 miles. Allow about 1½ hour.

The Burma Loop is a north-end road walk that is challenging and beautiful. It winds through forest above the Sound on Colvos Passage. Burma Rd. twists, rises, and drops amid typical Island forest land and ravines filled with sword ferns, salal and Oregon grape. There are homes on the road, and trails lead to residences on the waterfront, but these are private. Only one side road leads to the water.

Parking is available on SW Cedarhurst Rd., especially near 107th Way SW, and the walk may start any place on Cedarhurst Rd. Park well off the roadway and keep an eye out for on-coming cars, particularly on Burma Rd., which is one lane in some places.

Walk west toward Colvos Passage to Burma Rd. SW. Turn right onto Burma and stay right until reaching Vashon Hwy. SW. The walk is on the highway for 0.6 mi. before taking a right to return to SW Cedarhurst Rd., and back to the start.

DILWORTH LOOP

Includes two walks: 4.0 miles and 6.0 miles. Allow 1½ and 2½ hours

Dilworth/Glen Acres was one of the early communities serviced and accessed by water. The Reverend Dilworth used to hold camp meetings on the beach. At Point Beals was the Dilworth Dock, another Mosquito Fleet pickup point. Glen Acres once had a store, hotel, and dance hall. Its dock was another stopping point for the Mosquito Fleet. A small stand of large fir trees near Glen Acres helps walkers imagine how the Island's coastline might have appeared prior to settlement.

The Dilworth Loop Walk starts in town at Ober Park next to Vashon Hwy. SW. Park at or near the Vashon-Maury Parks District parking lot and walk north on Vashon

Hwy. SW, making a right on SW 171st St. This street heads east passing the Park and Ride, and soon the sewage treatment plant on the right. Follow the road which curves left and becomes 93rd Ave. SW. Turn right onto SW Gorsuch Rd., which makes a left bend and becomes 91st Ave. SW. The road goes by farmland and country homes. A number of these farms are members of the Vashon Island Growers' Association and are dedicated to the growth of organic produce and eggs.

Turn right onto SW Dilworth Rd., walking by more farmland, and follow the loop. It drops down to homes above the water on the eastside. While on Dilworth Rd. above the Sound, look for the fenced yard containing a bevy of small animals: goats, sheep, geese, Muscovy ducks, and various other charming animals. Be sure to look south; occasionally Mount Rainier comes into view. Stay on this road; it becomes SW Van Olinda Rd. and climbs back up the hill. Make the left turn onto 91st Ave. SW which leads back to Ober Park via the original route.

Total distance: 4.0 miles. Allow 1½ hours.

To add 2.0 miles to the Dilworth Loop, continue past Ober Park on the return walk, make a right at SW Bank Rd. and continue past shops, the fire station, and residences, turning right at 107th Ave. SW, right again at SW Cove Rd., and right again onto Vashon Hwy. SW. Continue back to Ober Park.

Total distance: 6.0 miles. Allow 2½ hours.

Pig Lane/Luana Beach Loop

Total distance: 5.6 miles. Allow 2½ hours. Elevation gain: About 500'.

This walk includes a good uphill workout and great views east to the mainland from the highest point.

Park at the south end of 75th Ave. SW at Dockton Rd. SW near the KING 5 towers. (Locally this stretch of 75th is called Pig Lane, after an old pig farm, to distinguish it from where 75th intersects Dockton Rd. south of SW 240th St.) Walk south on Dockton Rd., making a left turn onto SW 240th St. Follow 240th up the hill until it reaches SW Pt. Robinson Rd. On the right just before the top of the hill are the remains of a chicken farming operation. Colvos Creek Nursery is just east of this intersection.

Continue on Pt. Robinson Rd. east up and over the crest of the Island. In the past, this flat, now fairly clear crest, was wooded. A serious fire occurred in 1947, but because no one lived up here, it was allowed to burn until it went out. There are a number of farms, homes and estates along this high point of Maury Island.

Drop down the hill to where Pt. Robinson Rd. makes a "T" with SW Luana Beach Rd. Go left. Turning right at this point takes walkers to Point Robinson Park and the Point Robinson Lighthouse.

Luana Beach Rd. is a loop that drops to the waterfront on the north/northeast edge of Maury Island. The walk along the narrow road is noteworthy for older shoreline cottages. There are a number of bald eagles in the area to be spotted high in the tall firs.

Follow Luana Beach Rd. through wooded ravines climbing back up to Point Robinson Rd. and make a right. Be careful of traffic on this stretch. Walk west and make a left turn onto Pig Lane (75th Ave. SW) and head toward your cars. Along the lower stretch of Point Robinson Rd. were a number of strawberry fields.

REDDINGS BEACH LOOP

Total distance: 2.5–3.5 miles. Allow 1½ hours.

Park on SW 232nd St. near the south end of the private airfield and west of Old Mill Rd. SW. Walk west to Wax Orchard Rd. SW, go left, then, in a few hundred feet, right onto SW Reddings Beach Rd. Follow the loop, which becomes 147th SW and then SW 240th, all the way back to Wax Orchard Rd. SW, go left and return to the start on SW 232nd St.

Street Walks

Although a road walk, the off-the-main-road quietness of the loop is enjoyable. There is a nice view near the western part of the loop.

Total distance: 3.5 miles. Allow 1½ hours.

For a shorter walk, take the route to SW Reddings Beach Rd. and turn left on Landers Rd. SW off of Reddings Beach Rd. At SW 240th, go left back to Wax Orchard Rd. SW. and back to the start.

Total distance: 2.5 miles. Allow 1¼ hour.

THE DUCT TAPE DRILL (20 MILER)

Total distance: 20 miles. Allow around 7 hours.

A group of walkers training for a marathon put together this walk! The name, Duct Tape Drill, arose from the practice of wrapping duct tape around the feet to prevent blisters. This walk covers a lot of Island area, including forested land, a private airport, the cemetery and much up and down. This course travels past many eclectic homes, scenic meadowland, woods, ravines, and, of course, country roadways. Be sure to look for the famous "Bicycle in the Tree" to the north of the Sound Food building and, as always, watch for traffic.

Start at Sound Food resturant at the corner of Vashon Hwy. SW and SW 204th St., cross Vashon Hwy. and proceed west on SW 204th St. Make a right on 107th Ave. and a left on SW Cemetery Rd. This road, of course, passes the old Vashon Cemetery, established in 1888. Mary Gilman was the first white settler buried there in 1890. The cemetery is both historic and picturesque.

Follow Cemetery Rd., being sure to note the giant deer-shaped pond, cut into the lowland area by the Mann brothers (Ref. 14), south of the road shortly after the cemetery. Take the left fork onto Westside Hwy. SW. Don't go right toward the dump! Follow Westside Hwy. to SW 220th, turning right, then go left onto Wax Orchard Rd. Wax Orchard property has a private airstrip, and was a large and flourishing orchard. Today the family continues its food processing operation.

Walk south on Wax Orchard Rd. SW, take SW Reddings Beach Rd. and follow the loop back onto Wax Orchard Rd. Go right onto, and stay on, Wax Orchard Rd. to the intersection with Vashon Hwy. SW. Turn left back toward Burton. Stay on the highway to SW Burton Dr., making a left at the Burton store, Harbor Mercantile, and Back Bay Inn.

Burton is one of the Island's oldest settlements, and most of the buildings have a history. Back Bay Inn graces the SW corner with lodging and a restaurant. Harbor Mercantile serves the local as well as the boating community. A marina is located one block north near the post office. On the northwest corner of SW Burton Dr. and Vashon Hwy. SW is the old Masonic Lodge housing Silverwood Gallery downstairs and the Lodge upstairs. Across from the Masonic/Silverwood Building, an empty lot once held a combined drugstore, meat market, and small library. In the 1900s, the town had a high school and elementary school. The high school is gone, and the elementary school was demolished in 2003. Vashon College was built above Burton in the late 1800s, but burned in 1912 and was never rebuilt.

Heading west up the hill on SW Burton Rd., go right on 107th SW, left on SW 238th, right on 115th SW, left on SW 236th, right on Old Mill Rd. SW, left on SW 232nd and right onto Wax Orchard Rd. SW after you pass the private air strip. Go right on SW 220th and left onto Westside Hwy. SW. Follow the right fork onto SW Cemetery Rd., go right on 107th Ave. SW, left onto SW 204th and follow the home stretch back to Sound Food!

REFERENCES

1   Andrews, Jill A.B. and Kajira Wyn Berry, eds. *The Nature of an Island.* 2001. Vashon WA: Sand Dollar Press.

2   Carey, Roland. *Van Olinda's History of Vashon-Maury Island.* 1985. Seattle: Alderbrook Publishing Co.

3   *Beach Assessment Program 1995–1996, Using Volunteers to Survey Marine Shorelines in King County.* 1997. King County Dept. of Natural Resources.

4   Meeker, Helen, ed. *Parks and Recreation Open Space Plan for Vashon-Maury Islands—2001.* Vashon Park District. Available at Vashon Public Library.

5   *Vashon Island Trails—Property Maintenance Plan.* January 2002. King County Dept. of Natural Resources and Parks.

6   Campbell, Raymond S. and Reed Fitzpatrick. *Vashon & Maury Islands Map.* 1974. Vashon WA: Reed Fitzpatrick Forum Art Productions.

7   Private communication from Ann Spiers.

8   Swan, Ed. *The Birds of Vashon Island*, The Swan Company, 2005.

9   Silver, Nancy R. *A History of Vashon-Maury Island Re-addressed.* 2002. Vashon WA.

10 Waterman, T.T. *Puget Sound Geography.* Ed. with Additional Material from Vi Hilbert, Jay Miller, and Zalmai Zahir. 2001. Federal Way WA: Lushootseed Press.

11 Fox, Robert et al. *You and the Island.* Seattle: King County and Cooperative Extension Washington State U.

12 Waterman T.T. "Notes on the Ethnology of the Indians of Puget Sound." 1973. *Indian Notes and Mono-*

graphs #59. New York: Museum of the American Indian.

13 *Vashon-Maury Island Physical Characteristics/ Shoreline Inventory.* 1975. Seattle: King County Dept. of Community and Environmental Development.

14 Woodroffe, Pamela J. *Vashon Island's Agricultural Roots.* 2002. Lincoln NE: Writer's Club Press.

15 "Digging for Clues on Vashon Island—Burton Acres Shell Midden." *Completed Projects.* 2002. Seattle: University of Washington Burke Museum Website.

16 Stein, Julie K. and Laura S. Phillips. *Vashon Island Archaeology/A View from Burton Acres Shell Midden.* Burke Museum of Natural History and Culture. Seattle: University of Washington Press, 2003.

17 Buerge, David. *Curriculum Materials on Vashon-Maury Island Indians.* 1995. Unpublished but available at Vashon Public Library.

18 Chappell, Chris *Washington Natural heritage program site evaluation.* February 10, 1997. Available in Vashon Public Library.

19 Private communication from Gene Sherman.

THE AUTHORS

The authors are Islanders John Gerstle, a retired aerospace engineer, and Susan Sullivan, a retired biochemist. Both love to hike and walk. It is the authors' pleasure to share the numerous parks, trails and beach walks by providing a brief history and guide to this quiet, picturesque, funky island.